Next Step GUIDED READING *in Action*

View & Do Guide

Jan Richardson

SCHOLASTIC

ACKNOWLEDGEMENTS

Many thanks to the staff and teachers at Belmont Elementary School, Prince William County Public Schools, Woodbridge, VA, who helped make this video resource possible.

Special thanks to:

Bridget Outlaw, Principal; Michelle Rowe, Title 1 PWCS Supervisor; Kathy O'Hara, Title 1 Professional Development Specialist; Angela Karch and Sarah Bayne, Reading Specialists; Judy Collazo, Krista Connor, Kelly Schultz, Jennifer Matice, Michelle Dunphy, and Katie Edmond, lead teachers.

CREDITS

Online Resources featured text and images:

TRANSITIONAL

Henry's Freedom Box by Ellen Levine, illustrated by Kadir Nelson. Text copyright © 2007 by Ellen Levine. Illustrations copyright © 2007 by Kadir Nelson, Inc. Published by Scholastic Inc.
Chomp! A Book About Sharks by Melvin Berger. Text copyright © 2009 by Melvin Berger. Published by Scholastic Inc. Cover photograph © James D. Watt/Innerspace Visions.

FLUENT

"The Lobster and the Crab" and "The Ducks and the Fox" from *Fables* by Arnold Lobel. Copyright © 1980 by Arnold Lobel. Published by HarperCollins Children's Books, a division of HarperCollins Publishers.
"Landslide Disaster!" by Bob Woods from *SuperScience* magazine, October 2001. Copyright © 2001 by Scholastic Inc. Published by Scholastic Inc. Photographs © Carlos Leon/Reuters/Archive Photos.
"Thank You, Ma'am" by Langston Hughes featured in *Spotlight on... Point of View*. Compilation copyright © 2004 by Scholastic Inc. Published by Scholastic Inc. Used by permission. First published in *The Langston Hughes Reader* by Langston Hughes. Copyright © 1958 by Langston Hughes. Published by George Braziller, Inc., New York.
"Gilgamesh" from *Ancient Civilizations* by Wendy Conklin. Copyright © 2006 by Wendy Conklin. Published by Scholastic Inc.
"Paul Revere's Midnight Ride" by Henry Wadsworth Longfellow featured in *A Poem for Every Day* by Susan Moger. Copyright © 2006 by Susan Moger. Published by Scholastic Inc. First published in *The Atlantic Monthly*, January, 1861.
"The Unsinkable Molly Brown" text card from *Next Step Guided Reading Assessment, Grades 3–6*. Copyright © 2013 by Scholastic Inc. Published by Scholastic Inc.
All rights reserved.

Cover: Photo © GlobalStock/Getty Images

Common Core State Standards copyright © 2010. National Governors Association Center for Best Practices and Council of Chief State School Officers. All rights reserved.

Managing Editor: Sarah Longhi
Content Editor: Sarah Glasscock
Coordinating Video Producer: Shelley Griffin
Video Production Services by Seed Multimedia, LLC. Producer/Director: Kevin Carlson
Assistant Video Producer and Copyeditor: Lynne Wilson
Interior Design: Brian LaRossa
Cover Design: Maria Lilja

1 2 3 4 5 6 7 8 9 10   31   26 25 24 23 22 21 20 19 18 17

Contents

Introduction

I'm delighted you have chosen to view *Next Step Guided Reading in Action*. As I travel throughout America, I meet so many people who have purchased my book, *The Next Step in Guided Reading*, and want to know more about guided reading and what it can do for their students. They want to see an actual guided reading lesson and learn for themselves how this approach can transform their reading instruction. Well, I am extremely pleased to present these lessons to you so you can see how I personally plan and teach my guided reading lessons.

An effective guided reading lesson begins with knowing the readers. These videos will show you how I use assessments to determine students' strengths and needs, and how I select a focus for the group. With the focus in mind, I choose the text, plan my introduction, and prompt each student while he or she reads. For me, prompting individual students is the best part of guided reading. Making on-the-spot decisions in a side-by-side conversation with an individual student really takes reading instruction to the next level. I can differentiate my prompting and give each student just enough support to meet the challenge in the text.

I especially hope you will enjoy the narration. We included it so you can know what I was thinking when I planned and taught each lesson. After the lesson is over, I share what my next steps would be for the students in the group.

I love to teach guided reading . . . and I trust that comes through loud and clear in these videos. My hope is that you, too, will experience the joy of teaching students how to be better readers. Through guided reading you can help your students establish a strong literacy foundation that will sustain them in school and throughout their lives. Come alongside me as together we experience *Next Step Guided Reading in Action*.

THE GUIDED READING STAGES IN THE VIDEO

The following guided reading stages are featured in the videos online (available at scholastic.com/NSGRAction3UP) and in this guide:

▶ Transitional Readers

▶ Fluent Readers

You can view the video segments sequentially or watch them strategically. For example, if you have Transitional readers in your classroom, you can concentrate on that section, and then move to the Fluent section as your students progress.

Find your videos & downloadable forms at **scholastic.com/NSGRAction3UP**.

How to Use This Guide

This guide gives you the opportunity to reflect and act upon what you observe in the videos. Each guided reading stage in this guide and on the companion website is divided into five sections:

- ▶ Profile of a reader at that stage
- ▶ A step-by-step lesson plan
- ▶ Model lessons in action
- ▶ An individual conference
- ▶ Key teaching points

PROFILE This section provides an overview of the skills readers are developing at each stage. You'll also find information on appropriate texts to use with each stage. After viewing the video, you'll have a chance to think about and assess the readers in your classroom.

LESSON PLAN: STEP BY STEP In the guide, you'll see the framework of a lesson, with management tips about various aspects of guided reading, including group size and the amount of time recommended for each lesson component. After viewing the video, you'll have the tools to group your readers according to their needs and complete your own lesson plan for a group. Closing out this section is a list of the materials you'll need for your groups along with answers to common questions that teachers have asked me over the years.

MODEL LESSON IN ACTION This section of the guide shows the completed lesson plan I used to teach the model lesson in the video, including the observations I note about the students' performance. Keep this completed plan handy as you watch me teach the lesson. Additional details about each lesson component appear in the guide. After watching the lesson, you'll use a rubric to evaluate my lesson, and then you'll have a chance to review and refine your own lesson plan. (A printable version of each lesson plan is in this guide and also on the website.)

NAVIGATING THROUGH THE MODEL LESSON For the best understanding of how a guided reading lesson works, I recommend watching the Model Lesson videos from start to finish. Should you wish to focus on just one section of a lesson, you can navigate to the Before Reading, Read & Respond, or After Reading sections.

INDIVIDUAL CONFERENCE My observations and anecdotal notes during the small-group work alert me about students who are struggling with some aspect of the lesson. I then work one-on-one with these students to strengthen their use of the strategies and/or skills they are having difficulty with.

LESSON FRAMEWORK AND THE STANDARDS CHART Each guided reading stage in this guide concludes with a chart aligning lesson objectives with commonly held standards.

REPRODUCIBLES At the end of each stage in this guide, you'll find templates for the lesson plan that you can use to plan your own lessons. An icon in the guide will point you to the reproducible forms that appear on the accompanying website.

ASSESSING YOUR STUDENTS

Assessment is paramount to delivering effective guided reading instruction to your students. Effective assessment should help you answer the following questions:

▶ *How should I group my students?*

▶ *What text should I use with each group?*

▶ *What strategy should I teach?*

In the Profile and Lesson Plan: Step by Step sections, you'll find assessment guidance and support. I've also recently developed an all-in-one guided reading assessment with my colleague Maria Walther that will give you a complete snapshot of each student. This program will help you determine your students' instructional guided reading range and monitor their progress all year. I think you'll find it takes much less time to administer than some of the more cumbersome assessments you've used.

Next Step Guided Reading Assessment includes a brand-new leveled library complete with literary and informational texts that reflect the complexity recommended by the Common Core State Standards. For more information go to **www.scholastic.com/NextStepGuidedReading**.

NOTES

Transitional Readers

Average second-grade readers are at the transitional stage, but you will likely find readers at this level in any grade. Transitional readers have a large bank of sight words, but they are still learning to self-monitor, decode big words, increase fluency, expand vocabulary, and improve literal comprehension. The lessons in the video are appropriate for intermediate students who read between Levels J and P.

Instruction for Transitional Students	
Text Levels	**Instructional Needs**
J–P	• Self-monitoring
	• Decode multisyllabic words
	• Increase fluency
	• Expand vocabulary
	• Improve comprehension
	• Phonics: complex vowels, silent-*e* feature, words with more than two syllables

In this section, I'll demonstrate how to:

▶ Identify transitional readers
▶ Create a lesson plan for small groups of transitional readers
▶ Teach a small-group transitional lesson at Level M based on the lesson plan
▶ Teach a small-group transitional lesson at Level O based on the lesson plan
▶ Give a struggling reader more support in an individual conference
▶ Target key teaching points in the lesson

Profile of a Transitional Reader

Video Running Time: 2:32 | scholastic.com/NSGRAction3UP

Take a moment to look at the overview below and then view "Profile of a Transitional Reader."

Who is a transitional reader? Transitional readers are able to read at Levels J–P. Intermediate students who lag behind their peers are often transitional readers who need to improve decoding skills, vocabulary strategies, and comprehension. Once students are able to read and comprehend text at Level Q, they rarely have decoding and fluency issues, so they can advance to the fluent stage.

Text Reading at the Transitional Level

Transitional students will read texts at Levels J–P. Texts at the lower end are often short books with simple plots while higher-level texts may be longer with more elaborate themes and content. Be sure to include informational texts about topics of interest to your students.

My model transitional lesson plans on pages 16–19 and 20–23 use the following books:

Henry's Freedom Box
by Ellen Levine (Level M)

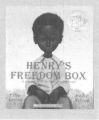

Chomp! A Book About Sharks
by Melvin Berger (Level O)

SUPPORT YOUR FOCUS STRATEGY Your primary goal in choosing a text for readers at any stage is finding one that supports your focus strategy.

REFLECTION

After you view the video, reflect on the students in your classroom who may be at the transitional stage.

ACTION

▶ First, assess your students. To analyze the strengths and needs of transitional readers, I have found the following types of assessments most useful:

• Running record with comprehension questions: A running record will help you select a text and focus strategy for your lesson. Administer it individually to identify each student's instructional reading level, reading strategies, and comprehension abilities. Have the student read aloud so you can record reading behaviors. Then ask the student to retell the text and answer comprehension questions.

- Word study inventory: Administer a word study inventory to the entire class to assess phonics skills. The inventory will identify the specific skills you should teach during the word study and guided writing components of your lesson. A Word Study Inventory for Transitional Readers reproducible is online.

- Anecdotal notes: Take notes on students' performance during small-group lessons and individual conferences.

▸ Record information from the assessments on the Assessment Summary Chart for Transitional Readers. A reproducible for the chart is on page 30, and directions for completing it are online.

▸ Use the Class Progress Chart to track the progress of your readers as they move from the transitional to the fluent stage.

Transitional Lesson Plan: Step by Step

Video Running Time: 8:14   scholastic.com/NSGRAction3UP

In this video, I explain how to plan and teach a transitional guided reading lesson. Before you view it, take a moment to look at the Transitional Lesson Framework below. The chart shows the components of a transitional guided reading lesson like the ones I teach in the video.

Transitional Lesson Framework	
DAY 1: Lesson Component	**DAY 2: Lesson Component**
Before Reading Gist statement introducing new book Preview text Teach new vocabulary Introduce and model strategy focus *(3–4 minutes)*	**Before Reading** Preview next section Teach new vocabulary *(2–3 minutes)*
Read & Respond Text Reading With Prompting *(10–12 minutes)*	**Read & Respond** Continue Reading With Prompting *(10–12 minutes)*
Teaching Points *(1–2 min)*	Teaching Points *(1–2 min)*
Discussion Prompt *(1–2 min)*	Discussion Prompt *(1–2 min)*
Word Study *(3–5 min)*	Word Study *(3–5 min)*
DAY 3: After Reading Rereading for Fluency *(optional: 5 minutes)* Guided Writing *(15–20 minutes)*	

For an in-depth explanation of the procedures for a transitional guided reading lesson, see pages 157–172 of *The Next Step in Guided Reading* (pages 175–202 in *The Next Step Forward in Guided Reading*).

TEACHING AN INDIVIDUAL TRANSITIONAL READER If you have a transitional reader who does not fit into any of your guided reading groups, teach him or her individually for ten minutes each day until the student accelerates and is able to join a group. You may also use the ten-minute lesson for a struggling reader who needs more scaffolding than you could provide in a small-group setting. For information on teaching an individual transitional lesson, see the "Ten-Minute Lesson for Transitional Readers" (Individual Instruction) online.

Download & Print!

TIME FRAME FOR A TRANSITIONAL GUIDED READING LESSON Allot about 20 minutes for a lesson. Using a timer and limiting teacher talk will help you pace your lesson and keep your students engaged and focused. It usually takes two or three days for transitional readers to finish a book.

THE TRANSITIONAL GUIDED READING GROUP Students one or two levels apart can be grouped together, but it's difficult to meet each student's needs if you have too many reading levels in one group. Transitional readers can be quite diverse. Some might have difficulty decoding but are able to recall; others may be fluent decoders but need to improve recall and retelling. The transitional lesson format provides for differentiated instruction because you can tailor your prompting and teaching points to individual students.

Continue to update your Assessment Summary Chart monthly and use the information to regroup students for guided reading. The average rate of progress for transitional students is one alphabetic level every 8–9 weeks.

REFLECTION

View "Transitional Lesson Plan: Step by Step" and reflect on the needs of the transitional students in your classroom. Consider how you will group them, then think about the lesson for each group:

▶ *Which transitional students are within one or two levels of each other?*

▶ *Which focus strategy will you use for each group: self-monitoring, decoding, fluency, vocabulary, or retelling?*

▶ *Which text supports the focus strategy?*

ACTION

▶ Complete an Assessment Summary Chart for Transitional Readers (page 30).

▶ Use your completed chart to select a focus for your lesson.

▶ Now it's time to fill out your own lesson plan. Use the Transitional Guided Reading Lesson Plan (page 31) to design a lesson plan for the group you've assembled.

▶ Review my explanation of each lesson component in the video as you work. Additional information appears on the next page.

❶ Introduce New Book/Continue Reading the Book

For Day 1, prepare a gist statement for the book. Introduce and model the focus strategy. Teach challenging words that students won't be able to decode on their own or are not defined in the text.

❷ Text Reading With Prompting

On Day 1, students begin to read the book independently with prompting from you. As you work with individual students, target your focus strategy but differentiate your prompting to meet each student's needs. For suggestions, see the Prompts for Guided Reading available online. On Day 2 (or possibly Day 3), students finish the book.

❸ Teaching Points

Refer to your anecdotal notes to choose one or two teaching points that match your students' needs: decoding strategies, vocabulary strategies, fluency and phrasing, and/or comprehension.

❹ Discussion Prompt

Each day, prepare a question that requires students to make inferences or draw conclusions about the story.

❺ Word Study

Do one activity that matches students' decoding/phonics needs. Use the Word Study Inventory from the website and your observations to determine your focus. Only transitional readers who need to work on decoding skills will need a word study activity.

❻ Guided Writing

Choose one of these response options after students read the book.

Transitional Guided Reading Lesson Plan (Levels J–P)

Title: _____ Level: _____ Strategy Focus: _____ Lesson #_____

❶
Day 1 Date_____ Pages_____	**Day 2** Date_____ Pages_____
Introduce New Book: This book is about	**Continue reading the book.** You will read about
New Vocabulary:	**New Vocabulary:**
Model Strategy:	**Observations:**

❷ Text Reading With Prompting (use prompts that are appropriate for each student).

❸ Teaching Points: Choose one or two each day (decoding, vocabulary, fluency, and/or comprehension).

Decoding Strategies:
- ☐ Reread & think what would make sense
- ☐ Cover (or attend to) the ending
- ☐ Use analogies
- ☐ Chunk big words

Fluency & Phrasing:
- ☐ Phrasing
- ☐ Attend to **bold** words
- ☐ Attend to punctuation
- ☐ Dialogue, intonation & expression

Vocabulary Strategies:
- ☐ Reread the sentence and look for clues
- ☐ Check the picture
- ☐ Use a known part
- ☐ Make a connection
- ☐ Use the glossary

Comprehension (oral):
- ☐ B-M-E   ☐ Problem & Solution
- ☐ S-W-B-S   ☐ Describe a character's feelings
- ☐ Who & What   ☐ STP (Stop Think Paraphrase)
- ☐ 5-Finger Retell   ☐ VIP (Very Important Part)
- Other:

❹
Discussion Prompt:	**Discussion Prompt:**

❺
Word Study (if appropriate): Sound boxes–Analogy chart–Make a big word	**Word Study (if appropriate):** Sound boxes–Analogy chart–Make a big word

❻ **Day 3 Reread the book for fluency (5 min.) and/or engage in Guided Writing (15–20 min.)**
Options for Guided Writing

Beginning-Middle-End	Five-Finger Retell	Somebody-Wanted-But-So	Character Analysis
Problem/Solution	Compare or Contrast	Event/Details	VIP
Chapter Summary	Cause/Effect	Main Idea/Details	

Other: _____

Materials You Will Need for a Transitional Lesson

For each group, gather the following materials:

- Dry-erase board, marker, and eraser (for you)
- Sets of lowercase magnetic letters or letter cards for word study (6 sets)
- Guided writing journals or reading notebooks (1 for each student)
- Assessment kit, which includes leveled reading passages, comprehension questions, and a word knowledge inventory
- Leveled books J–P, especially short fiction and informational texts written specifically for guided reading
- Sticky notes
- Timer

Reproducibles on the CD/online:

- Class Progress Chart
- Ten-Minute Lesson for Transitional Readers (Individual Instruction)
- Assessment Summary Chart for Transitional Readers (several copies): A reproducible also appears on page 30.
- Transitional Guided Reading Lesson Plan (several copies): A reproducible also appears on page 31.
- Word Study Inventory for Transitional Readers
- Personal Word Wall for Guided Writing (6 copies)
- Prompts for Guided Reading
- Question Cards (6 copies)
- Character Traits Chart (6 copies)
- Rubric for Transitional Guided Reading Lesson (Levels J–P)
- Problem-Solving Chart for Transitional Readers

Some Commonly Asked Questions

Do students always need to reread for fluency on Day 3? No. If students are fluent on Day 2, you can spend Day 3 entirely on guided writing.

How can I help students who have trouble with retelling? Teach them how to Stop, Think, and quietly Paraphrase (STP) each page as they read. If students have trouble retelling a page, remind them to use the picture as they STP. If they still cannot retell using picture support, choose an easier book. After students have read the entire book, have them take turns retelling a part of the story. If they get confused, prompt them to think about the pictures in the book.

What should I do while students read at the table? When students have decoding or fluency issues, listen to them read and prompt them accordingly. Then, when students are able to decode and read fluently, ask them to retell or engage them in a short conversation about what they've read. If students read fluently, retell with accuracy, and don't make errors, the book is too easy for them. When they are ready to work on deeper comprehension strategies, use the Fluent Lesson Plan on pages 61–62.

What if students need help spelling a word during guided writing? Should I tell them how to spell it? Always give students a copy of the Personal Word Wall to use during guided writing. A copy is online. It contains the 100 most frequently misspelled words, and you can add other words your students commonly misspell. If they need a word that is not on the list, you can direct them to use their books as a resource or teach them how to use a spelling feature from a word they already know. For example, if they need help spelling the *ou* part in *cloud*, have them write *out* and show them how the /ou/ sound in *out* is the same as the /ou/ sound in *cloud*. The final product may have some spelling errors, but it should be readable.

Does every transitional group need guided writing? Most transitional readers need to improve their writing skills. Guided writing is an excellent format for extending comprehension and teaching students how to become better writers. Additionally, reading and writing are reciprocal processes. What students learn in one area can be practiced and applied in the other.

Model Lesson in Action:
Transitional Reader Level M

Video Running Time: 29:48 | scholastic.com/NSGRAction3UP

In this video, I show what Day 1 of a transitional guided reading lesson at Level M looks and sounds like. This diverse group of five third graders is reading below grade level. Their monitoring and retelling skills are sound but only at a literal level. I chose the text *Henry's Freedom Box* by Ellen Levine so students can deepen their retelling by using inferential thinking to describe how the main character's feelings change over the course of the story.

VIEW ONLINE ▸ Take a moment to look at the completed lesson plan below and then view Day 1 of the lesson in the video. I suggest you print the corresponding completed Transitional Guided Reading Lesson Plan from the website and refer to it as you watch the lesson.

Transitional Guided Reading Lesson Plan (Levels J–P)

Title: *Henry's Freedom Box* Level: *M* Strategy Focus: Retell using character's feelings Lesson #____

Before Reading

Day 1 Date_____ Pages_____

Introduce New Book: This book is about a slave named Henry. RTFO what happened to him that caused him to risk his life for freedom.
Let's look through the pictures.

New Vocabulary: mistress, master, beckoned, tobacco, banjo.

Model Strategy: When you come to a sticky note, think about what happened on that page and how Henry felt.
Feeling words: excited, hopeful, thrilled, peaceful, disappointed, terrified, depressed, worried

Day 2 Date_____ Pages_____

Continue reading the book. You will read about Henry's journey to freedom. Use your list of character's feelings to describe Henry's reaction to events that occur.

New Vocabulary: crate, warehouse, vitriol, baggage car

Observations:

Read & Respond

Text Reading With Prompting (use prompts that are appropriate for each student).

Teaching Points: Choose one or two each day (decoding, vocabulary, fluency, and/or comprehension).

Decoding Strategies:
- ☐ Reread & think what would make sense
- ☐ Cover (or attend to) the ending
- ☐ Use analogies
- ☐ Chunk big words

Fluency & Phrasing:
- ☐ Phrasing
- ☐ Attend to **bold** words
- ☐ Attend to punctuation
- ☐ Dialogue, intonation & expression

Vocabulary Strategies:
- ☐ Reread the sentence and look for clues
- ☐ Check the picture
- ☐ Use a known part
- ☐ Make a connection
- ☐ Use the glossary

Comprehension (oral):
- ☐ B-M-E   ☐ Problem & Solution
- ☐ S-W-B-S   ☑ Describe a character's feelings
- ☐ Who & What   ☐ STP (Stop Think Paraphrase)
- ☐ 5-Finger Retell   ☐ VIP (Very Important Part)
- Other:

Discussion Prompt: How did Henry feel throughout the story? What happened to cause those feelings?
Discuss figurative language.
Mad minute: Write about Henry's feelings at the beginning of the story. Use events to tell why he was feeling that way.

Discussion Prompt: Share one of the feeling words you wrote down and talk about what events caused Henry to feel that way.
Turn and talk to your partner about what the author meant by "Henry's heart twisted in his chest."

Word Study (if appropriate): Sound boxes–Analogy chart–Make a big word

Word Study (if appropriate): Sound boxes–Analogy chart–Make a big word
oil   out
trail (ed) shout (ed)
paint (ed) mouth (ful)

After Reading

Day 3 Reread the book for fluency (5 min.) and/or engage in Guided Writing (15–20 min.)

Options for Guided Writing

Beginning-Middle-End	Five-Finger Retell	Somebody-Wanted-But-So	(Character Analysis)
Problem/Solution	Compare or Contrast	Event/Details	VIP
Chapter Summary	Cause/Effect	Main Idea/Details	

Other: Today you are going to retell the story using the feeling words you recorded on sticky notes. Be sure to include the events from the story that caused Henry to have those feelings

---

Day 1

BEFORE READING

To prepare, I flagged each student's copy of *Henry's Freedom Box* in places where I wanted them to record their inferences about the main character's feelings. To extend vocabulary, I created a chart on the chalkboard with feeling words that students could use during the lesson. I also wrote new vocabulary words on a whiteboard.

INTRODUCE NEW BOOK AND VOCABULARY

Introduce New Book: After reading aloud the title, I asked students to read the subtitle to help activate their background knowledge about the Underground Railroad.

Preview & Predict: As students previewed the text and made predictions based upon the illustrations, I brought up the focus strategy of the lesson: retell by tracking a character's feelings.

Introduce New Vocabulary: I introduced the new vocabulary words—*mistress*, *master*, *beckoned*, *tobacco*, and *banjo*—and discussed concepts that might be unfamiliar. We also discussed the following feeling words I'd written on a chart: (+) *excited, hopeful, thrilled, peaceful*; (–) *disappointed, terrified, depressed, worried*.

State the Focus Strategy: I modeled the focus strategy by reading aloud the first page and thinking aloud about the main character. Continuing to think aloud, I identified Henry's feelings as being in the negative column of the Feeling Words chart and decided on two words that would apply.

READ & RESPOND

TEXT READING WITH PROMPTING Students whisper-read the book independently while I conferred with each one individually. By tailoring my prompts, I was able to differentiate instruction for each student. For example, *Henry's Freedom Box* is filled with figurative language, and as I worked with Kendrick, I asked him about the phrase "his heart twisted in his chest" to make sure he understood what it revealed about Henry's feelings. As students read, I jotted down anecdotal notes. My notes for this group appear on page 19.

TEACHING POINTS After students had read for 10–15 minutes, I spent a few minutes working with the group on comprehension. Students took turns describing Henry's feelings, and the discussion gave me insight into their understanding of the text and the focus strategy.

DISCUSSION PROMPT To close the day's lesson, the group shared feeling words from their notes and gave text support for the feelings. Finally, I assigned a Mad Minute writing assignment in which students wrote about Henry's feelings at the beginning of the story.

WORD STUDY Because these students didn't need much work on their decoding or fluency skills, I did not give them a word study activity.

SUMMARY OF DAYS 2 AND 3

In the continuation of this lesson on Day 2, we did a quick review of the beginning of the book, and I gave a preview of what was to come. Before students began to read, I introduced a set of new vocabulary words: *crate*, *warehouse*, *vitriol*, and *baggage car*. Then the group continued to practice the focus strategy from Day 1, retelling using the character's feelings. Today, however, instead of asking them to use the chart I created, I handed out a copy of the Character Traits reproducible for them to use. As students read, I continued to prompt for retelling and decoding strategies.

On Day 2, I also asked them to complete an analogy chart (*oil/out*) for word study because I noticed on Day 1 that some students struggled to decode words with vowel patterns.

AFTER READING

GUIDED WRITING On Day 3, as a guided writing activity, students retold the story using the feeling words they recorded on their sticky notes. I reminded them to include the events that caused these feelings.

My observations from the three days of working with the group appear on the next page.

MY NOTES

Day 1: Introduce New Book Students did well with defining the feeling words from the chart.

Day 1: Decoding Strategies Covering up the -ed ending helped Hannah chunk *beckoned*.

Day 1: Vocabulary Strategies They used the illustrations and text to define *crate* and *warehouse*.

Day 1: Discussion Prompt Students referred to specific details in the text as they described the character's feelings. Some struggled with the figurative language.

Transitional Guided Reading Lesson Plan (Levels J–P)

Title: _Henry's Freedom Box_   Level: _m_   Strategy Focus: _Retell using characters' feelings_   Lesson # ___

Before Reading

Day 1 Date_____ Pages_____

Introduce New Book: This book is about _a slave named Henry. RTFO what happened to him that caused him to risk his life for freedom. Let's look through the pictures._

New Vocabulary: _mistress, master, beckoned, tobacco, banjo._

Model Strategy: _When you come to a sticky note, think about what happened on that page and how Henry felt. Feeling words: excited, hopeful, thrilled, peaceful, disappointed, terrified, depressed, worried_

Day 2 Date_____ Pages_____

Continue reading the book. You will read about _Henry's journey to freedom. Use your list of character's feelings to describe Henry's reaction to events that occur._

New Vocabulary: _crate, warehouse, vitriol, baggage car_

Observations:

Read & Respond

Text Reading With Prompting (use prompts that are appropriate for each student).

Teaching Points: Choose one or two each day (decoding, vocabulary, fluency, and/or comprehension).

Decoding Strategies:
- ☐ Reread & think what would make sense
- ☐ Cover (or attend to) the ending
- ☐ Use analogies
- ☑ Chunk big words

Vocabulary Strategies:
- ☐ Reread the sentence and look for clues
- ☑ Check the picture
- ☐ Use a known part
- ☐ Make a connection
- ☐ Use the glossary

Fluency & Phrasing:
- ☐ Phrasing
- ☐ Attend to **bold** words
- ☐ Attend to punctuation
- ☐ Dialogue, intonation & expression

Comprehension (oral):
- ☐ B-M-E
- ☐ S-W-B-S
- ☐ Who & What
- ☐ 5-Finger Retell
- ☐ Problem & Solution
- ☑ Describe a character's feelings
- ☐ STP (Stop Think Paraphrase)
- ☐ VIP (Very Important Part)
- Other:

Discussion Prompt: _How did Henry feel throughout the story? What happened to cause those feelings? Discuss figurative language._
Mad minute: Write about Henry's feelings at the beginning of the story. Use events to tell why he was feeling that way.

Discussion Prompt: _Share one of the feeling words you wrote down and talk about what events caused Henry to feel that way._
Turn and talk to your partner about what the author meant by "Henry's heart twisted in his chest."

Word Study (if appropriate): Sound boxes–Analogy chart–Make a big word

Word Study (if appropriate): Sound boxes–Analogy chart–Make a big word   _oil | out_   _brail(ed) shout(ed)_   _point(ed) mouth(ful)_

After Reading

Day 3 Reread the book for fluency (5 min.) and/or engage in Guided Writing (15–20 min.)

Options for Guided Writing

Beginning-Middle-End	Five-Finger Retell	Somebody-Wanted-But-So
Problem/Solution	Compare or Contrast	Event/Details
Chapter Summary	Cause/Effect	Main Idea/Details

(Character Analysis)   VIP

Other: _Today you are going to retell the story using the feeling words you recorded on sticky notes. Be sure to include the events from the story that caused Henry to have those feelings_

Observations

Day 1: Reduce scaffolding for Day 2. Use Character Trait Chart.

Day 2: Marbin needed support using the Character Trait Chart, so I'll schedule a one-on-one conference with him. Most students did well with less scaffolding.

Day 3: ELLs needed help with sentence structure. I'll encourage them to rehearse and reread each sentence.

Day 2: Discussion Prompt Students were more independent and confident during the discussion. The discussion of figurative language should continue.

Day 3: Guided Writing Students showed independence using vocabulary from the Character Trait Chart.

Model Lesson in Action: Transitional Reader Level O

Video Running Time: 29:24 | scholastic.com/NSGRAction3UP

In this video, I show what Day 1 of a transitional guided reading lesson at Level O looks and sounds like. This small group is composed of five third-grade students. They exhibit strong decoding and fluency skills, but they need to work on retelling. The text I chose is *Chomp! A Book About Sharks* by Melvin Berger because the title immediately engages students and the text offers lots of opportunities for asking questions, which is my focus strategy.

VIEW ONLINE ▶ Take a moment to look at the completed lesson plan below and then view Day 1 of the lesson in the video. I suggest you print the corresponding completed Transitional Guided Reading Lesson Plan from the website and refer to it as you watch the lesson.

Transitional Guided Reading Lesson Plan (Levels J–P)

Title: *Chomp!* Level: *O* Strategy Focus: *Ask questions + main idea/details* Lesson #____

Before Reading

Day 1 Date____ Pages____

Introduce New Book: This book is about *different kinds of sharks.*

Preview + Predict: *Read about why these sharks are considered to be great hunters.*

New Vocabulary:
lunges, frenzy, sleek

Model Strategy:
Ask and answer questions: literal (green) and inferential (red). Explain sticky notes. Strategy has already been modeled in class.

Day 2 Date____ Pages____

Continue reading the book. You will read about *more interesting facts about sharks and what makes them powerful swimmers.*

New Vocabulary:
gill slits, cartilage, remora

Observations:

Read & Respond

Text Reading With Prompting (use prompts that are appropriate for each student).

Teaching Points: Choose one or two each day (decoding, vocabulary, fluency, and/or comprehension).

Decoding Strategies:
- ☐ Reread & think what would make sense
- ☐ Cover (or attend to) the ending
- ☐ Use analogies
- ☐ Chunk big words

Vocabulary Strategies:
- ☐ Reread the sentence and look for clues
- ☑ Check the picture *remora*
- ☑ Use a known part *trusty*
- ☐ Make a connection
- ☐ Use the glossary

Fluency & Phrasing:
- ☐ Phrasing
- ☐ Attend to **bold** words
- ☐ Attend to punctuation
- ☐ Dialogue, intonation & expression

Comprehension (oral):
- ☐ B-M-E ☐ Problem & Solution
- ☐ S-W-B-S ☐ Describe a character's feelings
- ☐ Who & What ☐ STP (Stop Think Paraphrase)
- ☐ 5-Finger Retell ☐ VIP (Very Important Part)
- Other: *Ask + answer questions, main idea/details*

Discussion Prompt: *Students take turns asking + answering their questions. Why do sharks have a "feeding frenzy"?*

Mad Minute: *Why is the shark a great hunter?*

Discussion Prompt: *Use your details to retell what you learned about the shark (fin, scales, cartilage). How did the photos help you identify some important details about this chapter? How do the scales help the shark swim fast? What would happen if the shark stopped swimming?*

Word Study (if appropriate): *N/A*
Sound boxes–Analogy chart–Make a big word

Word Study (if appropriate): *N/A*
Sound boxes–Analogy chart–Make a big word

After Reading

Day 3 Reread the book for fluency (5 min.) and/or engage in Guided Writing (15–20 min.)

Options for Guided Writing

Beginning-Middle-End	Five-Finger Retell	Somebody-Wanted-But-So	Character Analysis
Problem/Solution	Compare or Contrast	Event/Details	VIP
Chapter Summary	Cause/Effect	(Main Idea/Details)	

Other:
1. *Turn the heading into a question.*
2. *Answer the question.*
3. *Give examples using important details from the chapter.*
4. *Write an "I wonder…" statement.*

Day 1

BEFORE READING

Before the group met, I used information on the Assessment Summary Chart and my discussion with their teacher to decide which students should ask questions that require inferential thinking and which should ask questions that deal with literal comprehension.

To prepare for the lesson, I placed green flags in the book for students who would ask literal questions, and red flags for those who would ask inferential questions. As an additional scaffold, I gave each student a Question Card that included appropriate question starters. I also wrote the new vocabulary words on a small whiteboard.

INTRODUCE NEW BOOK AND VOCABULARY

Introduce New Book: Notice how simple and brief my introduction is. I just stated the title and had students preview the book.

Preview & Predict: I gave students a few minutes to look at the pictures in the text and discuss them with a partner. Then we read the title of Chapter One, "Great Hunters," and I told students what the chapter would be about.

Introduce New Vocabulary: The words I introduced and defined were *lunges*, *frenzy*, and *sleek*. Notice how I said each word and offered a simple definition, connected it to students' background knowledge, and related it to the text. I also had them discuss each word with a partner.

INTRODUCE AND MODEL STRATEGY

State the Focus Strategy: Although the Asking Questions strategy is a comprehension strategy from the Fluent Lesson Plan, these students know the strategy because it has been introduced and modeled in a whole-class lesson. I quickly reviewed the concept of asking green and red questions and pointed out the flags in their copies of *Chomp!* I also briefly reviewed where they would find the answers to their questions: in the book (green) or in their head (red).

READ & RESPOND

TEXT READING WITH PROMPTING On each day of the lesson, students whisper-read the book independently while I conferred with individuals. By tailoring my prompts, I was able to differentiate instruction. For example, Carla needed help writing a question, so I prompted her to take a fact from the page and use the question starter "where" to turn the fact into a question. As students read, I jotted down anecdotal notes. My notes for this group appear on page 23.

TEACHING POINTS After students had read for 10–15 minutes, I spent a few minutes working with the group on comprehension. Using the focus strategy of asking questions gave me insight into each student's comprehension.

DISCUSSION PROMPT In this lesson, I assigned a Mad Minute as the discussion prompt. For one minute, students wrote one fact they learned that explained why sharks are great hunters. Then they shared their work. Retelling a fact reinforced their comprehension of the text.

WORD STUDY Because these students didn't need to work on their decoding or fluency skills today, I did not give them a word study activity.

SUMMARY OF DAYS 2 AND 3

On Day 2, students read the second chapter of *Chomp!* After sharing a brief gist statement of the chapter and introducing new vocabulary, I modeled a new focus strategy, main idea, and details to move students even deeper into the text. They built on the focus strategy from Day 1 by turning the main idea—the chapter title "Powerful Swimmers"—into a question and identifying a key detail as a response. They then used the details to discuss what they learned in the chapter. Based on their performance on Day 2, I made a recommendation to their teacher for the next step in their instruction.

AFTER READING

GUIDED WRITING On Day 3, as a guided writing activity, students selected a chapter from the book and turned the title into a question. That became the first sentence in their paragraph. Then they wrote a few sentences that answered the question, harvesting important details from their notes and the book. They closed their paragraph by writing an "I wonder . . ." statement about something they learned in that chapter.

My observations from the three days of working with this group appear on the next page.

My Notes

Day 1: New Vocabulary
Students did well explaining the new vocabulary to their partner. When Eduardo had difficulty decoding *appetite*, I asked everyone to stop reading so I could explain its meaning and add it to the new vocabulary words.

Teaching Points: Vocabulary Strategies
Students used pictures to clarify new vocabulary. They needed support using a known part of a word.

Day 1: Discussion Prompt Carla and Eduardo struggled to answer inferential questions. Most students did well answering literal questions. They understood the main idea of the chapter.

Observations
Day 1: Most students needed some support in order to ask questions about the text.

Day 2: Most students were independent with determining important details.

Teaching Points: Fluency & Phrasing
I recommend buddy-reading to strengthen Eduardo's fluency—about 20–30 minutes of easy reading every day.

Day 2: Discussion Prompt Students didn't understand how the sharks' smooth scales help them swim fast. They were able to find key details in the chapter. Next Step: using the title and key details to summarize a chapter.

Day 3: Guided Writing Students did well using their notes and text features to write a paragraph that summarized one chapter. They used spelling resources but needed prompting for punctuation. I supported Eduardo with syntax.

Transitional Guided Reading Lesson Plan (Levels J–P)

Title: _Chomp!_ Level: _O_ Strategy Focus: _Ask questions + main idea/details_ Lesson #_____

Before Reading

Day 1 Date_____ Pages_____

Introduce New Book: This book is about _different kinds of sharks._
Preview + Predict: _Read about why these sharks are considered to be great hunters._

New Vocabulary:
lunges, frenzy, sleek

Model Strategy:
Ask and answer questions: literal (green) and inferential (red)
Explain sticky notes. Strategy has already been modeled in class.

Day 2 Date_____ Pages_____

Continue reading the book. You will read about _more interesting facts about sharks and what makes them powerful swimmers._

New Vocabulary:
gill slits, cartilage, remora

Observations:

Read & Respond

Text Reading With Prompting (use prompts that are appropriate for each student).

Teaching Points: Choose one or two each day (decoding, vocabulary, fluency, and/or comprehension).

Decoding Strategies:
- ☐ Reread & think what would make sense
- ☐ Cover (or attend to) the ending
- ☐ Use analogies
- ☐ Chunk big words

Fluency & Phrasing:
- ☐ Phrasing
- ☐ Attend to **bold** words
- ☐ Attend to punctuation
- ☐ Dialogue, intonation & expression

Vocabulary Strategies:
- ☐ Reread the sentence and look for clues
- ☑ Check the picture _remora_
- ☑ Use a known part _trusty_
- ☐ Make a connection
- ☐ Use the glossary

Comprehension (oral):
- ☐ B-M-E   ☐ Problem & Solution
- ☐ S-W-B-S   ☐ Describe a character's feelings
- ☐ Who & What   ☐ STP (Stop Think Paraphrase)
- ☐ 5-Finger Retell ☐ VIP (Very Important Part)
- Other: _Ask + answer questions; Main idea/details_

Discussion Prompt: _Students take turns asking + answering their questions. Why do sharks have a "feeding frenzy?"_
Mad Minute: Why is the shark a great hunter?

Discussion Prompt: _Use your details to retell what you learned about the shark (fin, scales, cartilage). How did the photos help you identify some important details about this chapter? How do the scales help the shark swim fast? What would happen if the shark stopped swimming?_

Word Study (if appropriate): _N/A_
Sound boxes–Analogy chart–Make a big word

Word Study (if appropriate): _N/A_
Sound boxes–Analogy chart–Make a big word

After Reading

Day 3 Reread the book for fluency (5 min.) and/or engage in Guided Writing (15–20 min.)
Options for Guided Writing

Beginning-Middle-End	Five-Finger Retell	Somebody-Wanted-But-So	Character Analysis
Problem/Solution	Compare or Contrast	Event/Details	VIP
Chapter Summary	Cause/Effect	(Main Idea/Details)	

Other:
1. Turn the heading into a question.
2. Answer the question.
3. Give examples using important details from the chapter.
4. Write an "I wonder..." statement.

Target Skills and Strategies

For more information on the following skills and strategies, see these "Teaching Points" video clips:

- **Make Connections to Known Words:** Drawing an analogy to a known word can aid a student in decoding an unknown word. In the video, I prompt a student to connect *five*, a word he knows, to a part of *arrive*.

- **Improve Comprehension With Character Analysis:** Asking questions about a character can lead students to higher-level thinking about a text.

- **Turn a Fact Into a Question to Improve Comprehension:** A fact from the text can be turned into a literal inferential question.

- **Focus on Details and Main Idea to Build Comprehension:** Turning a fact into a question can help students identify the main idea and supporting details.

- **Introduce New Vocabulary in Four Steps:** If there is no text support for determining a word's meaning, define the word, connect it to students' background, relate it to the text, and have them turn and talk about it.

- **Use Vocabulary Strategies to Define New Words:** Useful strategies for defining new words include looking for clues in illustrations and using a known part of an unfamiliar word.

REFLECTION

Take time to evaluate my model lesson plans. Based on what you saw, would you make any changes in your lesson plan?

ACTION

- ▶ Complete the Rubric for Transitional Guided Reading Lesson (Levels J–P) to evaluate the components of each of my lesson plans.

- ▶ Review and refine your lesson plan.

- ▶ Teach your lesson. Remember to record your observations and notes to assess your students' performance and progress.

Individual Conference: Struggling Reader

Video Running Time: 5:06 | *scholastic.com/NSGRAction3UP*

Problem areas for transitional readers include motivation, self-monitoring, decoding, fluency, vocabulary, and retelling.

ADDRESSING MOTIVATION

One reason struggling readers don't like to read is that they can't find appropriately leveled books that interest them. Here are some suggestions for motivating reluctant readers:

▸ Use the information you collect from your observations during independent reading to help these students find engaging, level-appropriate books. Make a big deal about selecting books "just for them" because you think they will enjoy them. Ask them to let you know if they don't like a book so you can help them find a different one.

▸ Have students read with a buddy from the classroom. Show them how to sit beside each other and either read silently or take turns reading softly.

▸ Encourage students to participate in Readers' Theater. Because they will perform in front of the class, they will be forced to reread the text several times. Be sure to choose a text at the student's independent reading level.

▸ Have another adult—a student teacher, instructional aid, or parent volunteer—do neurological impress with the student for 15 minutes a day for at least 21 days. For more information on this method, see page 264 in *The Next Step in Guided Reading* (page 212 in *The Next Step Foward in Guided Reading*).

▸ Let students listen to a recorded story. I recommend this only as a last resort because a struggling reader often has a difficult time keeping up with the reading speed on the recording. Still, I would rather have a student listen to a story than do nothing. Hearing the story may eventually motivate the student to read the book on his or her own.

ADDRESSING PROCESSING PROBLEMS

For steps you can take to address problems with self-monitoring, spelling, phonics skills, fluency, vocabulary, and retelling, see the Problem Solving Chart for Transitional Readers available online.

After working with Marbin in the small group and consulting with his teacher, I decided to work with him individually. To see me teach decoding strategies, watch the "Individual Conference" video.

State the Purpose of the Conference

It's important to begin a one-on-one conference with specific praise and then state your purpose for the conference. In the video, I pointed out how well Marbin did remembering the story, and then I explained that I was going to teach him some strategies for decoding.

USE A KNOWN PART Marbin had difficulty decoding the word *crate*, so I prompted him to see if he could use a part he knew, *ate*.

PRAISE FOR SELF-MONITORING Initially, Marbin read *now* instead of *how*, but he self-corrected and read the word accurately. I praised Marbin for noticing his error. If he had not corrected the error, I would have waited until he had finished the sentence and asked, "Does that make sense?"

COVER THE ENDING Marbin made a couple of miscues for *lifted*. On his first try, he said *felt*, but made another error when he corrected it to *lefted*. I prompt him to tell me about his thinking. His response and gesture indicated he thought the word was *left*, not *lift*. When working with second language learners, it is always a good idea to check their understanding of vocabulary. I guided Marbin to cover the ending *-ed* to focus on *lift*, which helped him to decode the word and determine its meaning. Once a student correctly reads a word, it's important to have him or her reread the entire sentence.

CHECK THE PICTURE Although we already used the "known part strategy" to read *crate*, I asked Marbin to point out the crate in the illustration to check his understanding of the word. Illustrations are often a valuable tool for deciphering the meaning of new words.

CHUNK THE WORD Marbin didn't stumble over the word *warehouse*, but I wanted to see if he understood how to chunk a big word into parts. His response to my question showed that he not only knew how to chunk the word, but that he also understood its meaning.

Follow-up

After an individual conference, continue to monitor the student during guided reading lessons. In a few weeks, arrange another conference to evaluate his or her progress and determine the next step in instruction.

The Transitional Guided Reading Lesson Framework: Addressing Standards

The chart below shows how each component of the Transitional Lesson Framework aligns with commonly held state and national standards.*

Transitional Lesson Component/ Objective	*Standards
Before Reading	
Introduce New Book New Vocabulary Model Strategy	**LITERATURE** **Integration of Knowledge and Ideas:** **3.7** Explain how specific aspects of a text's illustrations contribute to what is conveyed by the words in a story. **4.7** Make connections between the text of a story and a visual presentation of the text, identifying where each version reflects specific descriptions and directions in the text. **5.7** Analyze how visual elements contribute to the meaning, tone, or beauty of a text. **INFORMATIONAL TEXT** **Integration of Knowledge and Ideas:** **3.7** Use information gained from illustrations and the words in a text to demonstrate understanding of the text. **4.7** Interpret information presented visually and explain how the information contributes to an understanding of the text in which it appears.
Read & Respond	
Text Reading With Prompting: • Self-monitoring • Decoding • Fluency • Vocabulary • Comprehension Teaching Points: • Decoding • Fluency & Phrasing • Vocabulary • Comprehension	**LITERATURE** **Key Ideas and Details:** **3.1** Ask and answer questions to demonstrate understanding of a text, referring explicitly to the text as the basis for the answers. **3.3** Describe characters in a story and explain how their actions contribute to the sequence of events. **4.1** Refer to details in a text when explaining what the text says explicitly and when drawing inferences from the text. **4.3** Describe in depth a character, setting, or event in a story, drawing on specific details in the text. **5.1** Quote accurately from the text when explaining what the text says explicitly and when drawing inferences from the text. **5.3** Compare and contrast two or more characters, settings, or events in a story, drawing on specific details in the text.

Craft and Structure:

3.4 Determine the meaning of words and phrases as they are used in a text, distinguishing literal from nonliteral language.

3.6 Distinguish their own point of view from that of the narrator or those of the characters.

4.4 Determine the meaning of words and phrases as they are used in a text, including those that allude to significant characters found in mythology.

4.6 Compare and contrast the point of view from which different stories are narrated, including the difference between first- and third-person narratives.

5.4 Determine the meaning of words and phrases as they are used in a text, including figurative language such as metaphors and similes.

5.6 Describe how the narrator's or speaker's point of view influences how events are described.

Integration of Knowledge and Ideas:

3.7 Explain how specific aspects of a text's illustrations contribute to what is conveyed by the words in a story.

Range of Reading and Level of Text Complexity:

3.10 By the end of the year, read and comprehend literature, including stories, dramas, and poetry, at the high end of the grades 2–3 text complexity band independently and proficiently.

4.10 By the end of the year, read and comprehend literature, including stories, dramas, and poetry, in the grades 4–5 text complexity band proficiently, with scaffolding as needed at the high end of the range.

5.10 By the end of the year, read and comprehend literature, including stories, dramas, and poetry, at the high end of the grades 4–5 text complexity band independently and proficiently.

INFORMATIONAL TEXT

Key Ideas and Details:

3.1 Ask and answer questions to demonstrate understanding of a text, referring explicitly to the text as the basis for the answers.

3.2 Determine the main idea of a text; recount the key details and explain how they support the main idea.

4.1 Refer to details and examples in a text when explaining what the text says explicitly and when drawing inferences from the text.

4.2 Determine the main idea of a text and explain how it is supported by key details; summarize the text.

5.1 Quote accurately from a text explaining what the text says explicitly and when drawing inferences from the text.

5.2 Determine two or more main ideas of a text and explain how they are supported by key details; summarize the text.

Craft and Structure:

3.4 Determine the meaning of general academic and domain-specific words and phrases in a text relevant to a grade 3 topic or subject area.

3.5 Use text features and search tools to locate information relevant to a given topic efficiently.

3.6 Distinguish their own point of view from that of the author of a text.

4.4 Determine the meaning of general academic and domain-specific words and phrases in a text relevant to a grade 4 topic or subject area.

5.4 Determine the meaning of general academic and domain-specific words and phrases in a text relevant to a grade 5 topic or subject area.

Integration of Knowledge and Ideas:
3.7 Use information gained from illustrations and the words in a text to demonstrate understanding of the text.
4.7 Interpret information presented visually and explain how the information contributes to an understanding of the text in which it appears.
Range of Reading and Levels of Text Complexity:
3.10 By the end of the year, read and comprehend informational texts, including history/social studies, science, and technical texts, at the high end of the grades 2–3 text complexity band independently and proficiently.
4.10 By the end of the year, read and comprehend informational texts, including history/social studies, science, and technical texts, in the grades 4–5 text complexity band proficiently, with scaffolding as needed at the high end of the range.
5.10 By the end of the year, read and comprehend informational texts, including history/social studies, science, and technical texts, at the high end of the grades 4–5 text complexity band independently and proficiently.

Discussion Prompt

LITERATURE
Key Ideas and Details:
3.1 Ask and answer questions to demonstrate understanding of a text, referring explicitly to the text as the basis for the answers.
4.1 Refer to details in a text when explaining what the text says explicitly and when drawing inferences from the text.
5.1 Quote accurately from the text when explaining what the text says explicitly and when drawing inferences from the text.

INFORMATIONAL TEXT
Key Ideas and Details:
3.1 Ask and answer questions to demonstrate understanding of a text, referring explicitly to the text as the basis for the answers.
4.1 Refer to details and examples in a text when explaining what the text says explicitly and when drawing inferences from the text.
5.1 Quote accurately from a text explaining what the text says explicitly and when drawing inferences from the text.

Word Study

FOUNDATIONAL
Phonics and Word Recognition:
3.3, **4.3**, **5.3** Know and apply grade-level phonics and word analysis skills in decoding words.

After Reading

Guided Writing

Range of Writing:
3.10, **4.10**, **5.10** Write routinely over . . . short time frames (a single sitting or a day or two) for a range of discipline-specific tasks, purposes, and audiences.

*The Common Core State Standards are used here as a point of reference.

Name	Inst. Level	Monitors for Meaning + ✔ -	Decodes + ✔ -	Fluency (1–4)	Retell + ✔ -		Needs Word Study Check (✔) areas that need to be taught.			
					F	NF	vowels	digraphs	blends	endings

(Fountas & Pinnell Levels J–P)

Monitors for Meaning: (+) always, (✔) sometimes, (–) rarely

Decodes: (+) Uses beginning, medial, and inal letters; attends to parts and endings; (✔) Uses beginning and inal letters; ignores medial sounds and some endings; (–) Uses some letter sounds; not consistent in attending to visual cues

Fluency: 4 = phrased & fluent with expression; 3 = phrased but without intonation, ignores some punctuation; 2 = mostly two-word phrases; 1 = word by word

Retell: (+) complete, (✔) partial, (–) very limited/weak

Needs Word Study: Use the Word Study Inventory to determine phonics needs.

Transitional Guided Reading Lesson Plan (Levels J–P)

Title: _____ Level: _____ Strategy Focus: _____ Lesson #_____

Day 1 Date_____ Pages_____	**Day 2** Date_____ Pages_____
Introduce New Book: This book is about	**Continue reading the book.** You will read about
New Vocabulary:	**New Vocabulary:**
Model Strategy:	**Observations:**

Text Reading With Prompting (use prompts that are appropriate for each student). See page 295.

Teaching Points: Choose one or two each day (decoding, vocabulary, fluency, and/or comprehension).

Decoding Strategies:	**Fluency & Phrasing:**
❑ Reread & think what would make sense	❑ Phrasing
❑ Cover (or attend to) the ending	❑ Attend to **bold** words
❑ Use analogies	❑ Attend to punctuation
❑ Chunk big words	❑ Dialogue, intonation & expression

Vocabulary Strategies:	**Comprehension** (oral):	
❑ Reread the sentence and look for clues	❑ B-M-E	❑ Problem & Solution
❑ Check the picture	❑ S-W-B-S	❑ Describe a character's feelings
❑ Use a known part	❑ Who & What	❑ STP (Stop Think Paraphrase)
❑ Make a connection	❑ 5-Finger Retell	❑ VIP (Very Important Part)
❑ Use the glossary	Other:	

Discussion Prompt:	**Discussion Prompt:**

Word Study (if appropriate):	**Word Study (if appropriate):**
Sound boxes–Analogy chart–Make a big word	Sound boxes–Analogy chart–Make a big word

Day 3   Reread the book for fluency (5 min.) and/or engage in Guided Writing (15–20 min.)

Options for Guided Writing

Beginning-Middle-End	Five-Finger Retell	Somebody-Wanted-But-So	Character Analysis
Problem/Solution	Compare or Contrast	Event/Details	VIP
Chapter Summary	Cause/Effect	Main Idea/Details	

Other: _____

Fluent Readers

By the end of the third grade, most intermediate students reading on grade level are fluent readers. The lesson plans I teach in the video are appropriate for students who read text at Levels Q and above.

Instruction for Fluent Students	
Text Levels	**Instructional Needs**
Q and above	• Increasing vocabulary • Using a variety of comprehension strategies

In this section, I'll demonstrate how to:

▶ Identify fluent readers
▶ Create a lesson plan for small groups of fluent readers
▶ Teach two small-group fluent lessons at Level S based on lesson plans
▶ Teach a small-group fluent lesson at Level U based on the lesson plan (lesson highlights only)
▶ Give a struggling student more support in an individual conference
▶ Target key teaching points in a lesson

Profile of a Fluent Reader

Video Running Time: 2:05 | scholastic.com/NSGRAction3UP

 Take a moment to look at the overview below and then view "Profile of a Fluent Reader."

Who is a fluent reader? Fluent readers are good decoders who are able to explore the deeper levels of comprehension by reading challenging texts. Aided by teacher scaffolding, fluent readers learn a variety of comprehension strategies to understand complex texts. Scaffolding should decrease as they begin to independently apply the strategies.

Text Reading at the Fluent Level

Fluent students will read texts at Level Q and above. Use a variety of texts including poetry, short stories, short chapter books, newspaper and magazine articles, and other informational texts about topics of interest to students. The key is to offer a text with the right amount of challenge.

My model fluent lesson plans on pages 41–52 focus on the following books:

"The Lobster and the Crab," a fable by Arnold Lobel	"Landslide Disaster!," a nonfiction article by Bob Woods	"Thank You, Ma'm," a short story by Langston Hughes

 SUPPORT YOUR FOCUS STRATEGY Your primary goal in choosing a text for readers at any stage is finding one that supports your focus strategy.

REFLECTION

After you view the video, reflect on the students in your classroom who may be at the fluent stage.

ACTION

▶ First, assess your students.

- Administer a running record with comprehension questions. Use a leveled passage and have students read it silently. Then ask each student to give you an oral retell and respond to some questions about the passage.

- Also use your observations of students' responses during small-group lessons and individual conferences, as well as your anecdotal records.

▶ Record information from the assessments on the Assessment Summary Chart for Fluent Readers. A reproducible of the chart and directions for completing it are on the website.

Fluent Lesson Plan: Step by Step

Video Running Time: 6:15 | *scholastic.com/NSGRAction3UP*

In this video, I explain how to plan and teach a fluent guided reading lesson. The chart below shows the components of a lesson like the ones I teach in the video.

Fluent Lesson Framework		
Before Reading	**Read & Respond**	**After Reading**
Introduction	Model Strategy	Discussion
Preview & Predict	*(1 minute) Day 1 Only*	Teaching Points
(3–4 minutes) Day 1 Only	Conference with students	• Decoding
New Vocabulary	as they read and respond	• Vocabulary
(1–2 minutes)	*(10 minutes)*	• Comprehension
		(5 minutes)
		Words for New Word List
		(1 minute)
After Reading Entire Text		
Guided Writing		
(optional: 20 minutes)		

For an in-depth explanation of the procedures for a fluent guided reading lesson, see pages 189–198 of *The Next Step in Guided Reading* (pages 235–250 of *The Next Step Forward in Guided Reading*).

THE FLUENT GUIDED READING GROUP The Assessment Summary Chart for Fluent Readers makes it easy to group students, based on the strategy focus. The bottom line is this: Know your students and teach them what they need to learn to become better readers. About once a month, re-evaluate your groups by reviewing the anecdotal notes you've taken during guided reading lessons. I recommend no more than six students in a group so you have time to confer with each one.

REFLECTION

View "Fluent Lesson Plan: Step by Step" and reflect on the needs of the fluent readers in your classroom. Consider how you will group them, then think about the lesson for each group:

> ▶ *Which fluent readers need to work on the same skill and/or strategy?*
>
> ▶ *Which focus strategy will you use with each group?*
>
> ▶ *What genre would best support the focus strategy?*
>
> ▶ *Which text in that genre would provide enough challenge and support the focus strategy?*
>
> ▶ *How many days will it take for the group to read the entire text?*

ACTION

► Complete the Assessment Summary Chart for Fluent Readers. You can review my completed charts for two groups in the video.

► Use your completed chart to ensure that your groupings meet your students' needs.

► Now it's time to fill out your own lesson plan. Use both pages of the Fluent Guided Reading Lesson Plan on pages 61–62 to design a lesson plan for one group you've targeted.

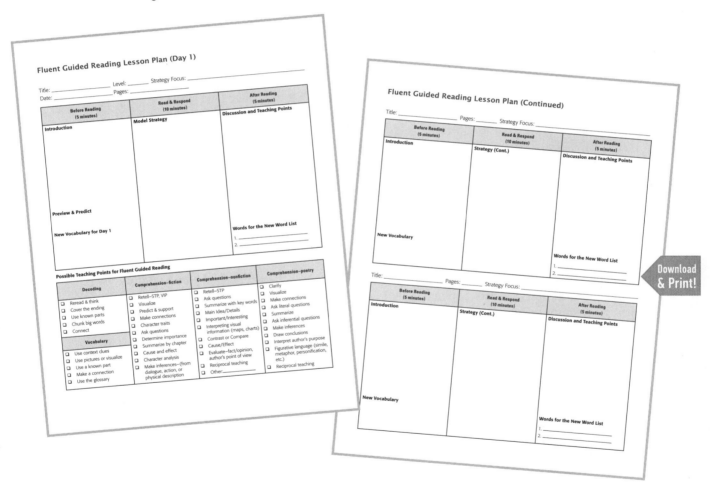

► Review my explanation of each lesson component in the video as you work. Additional information appears on the next page.

① BEFORE READING

Decide which sections of the text to read and discuss each day. For Day 1, prepare a gist statement that gives students a general overview of the text. Then help them preview the illustrations, headings, and other text features to make predictions and ask questions about what they will read. Model the focus strategy. Decide how you will scaffold your students as they practice the strategy. Introduce vocabulary not defined in the text.

② READ & RESPOND

Students begin to read the book independently with prompting from you. On subsequent days, they finish the book. As you have individual conferences, focus on the target strategy but differentiate your instruction to meet each student's needs.

③ AFTER READING

For each day of a lesson, write a thought-provoking question to lift the processing level of your students.

④ POSSIBLE TEACHING POINTS

Place a checkmark by the teaching points you want to use during and after reading. There are three levels of comprehension strategies: literal (retell), interpretive (inferences, comparisons and contrasts), and evaluative (evaluate author's purpose or form an opinion about the text).

⑤ WORDS FOR THE NEW WORD LIST

On Day 1, select two words from the passage for the students to add to their New Word List. Choose high-utility words or words that provide opportunities to teach word-analysis skills.

⑥ SUBSEQUENT DAYS

Repeat Day 1 procedures for the next sections of the text. Continue until the text is completed. You may then choose to do a Guided Writing activity to extend comprehension and support struggling writers. Some suggestions appear on the next page.

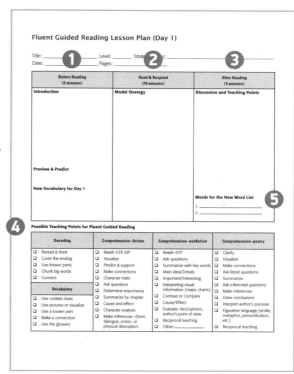

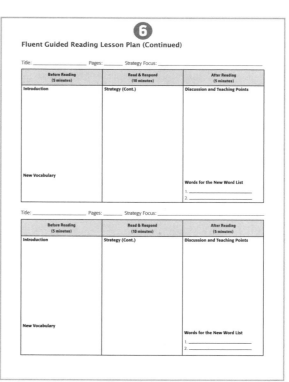

Guided Writing Activities

Fiction

- Describe a character drawing on specific details in the text.
- Summarize the story.
- Compare and contrast characters from the same story.
- Compare and contrast characters, settings, themes, points of view, etc., of two different stories.
- Write a poem from a character's point of view.
- Explain a theme in the story.

Informational

- Summarize a chapter or section using the main idea and key details.
- Use the index to find important concepts to compare and contrast.
- Write about the causes and effects of historical events.
- Write a poem about a famous person, drawing from important events in his or her life.
- Write about the topic by integrating information from several texts.
- Compare your point of view with that of the author.

Poetry

- Make connections to the poem.
- Summarize the poem.
- Explain a literary element the poet used.
- Describe how the poet used specific words to create mood.
- Compare and contrast themes, points of view, mood, etc., of two poems.

Materials You Will Need for the Fluent Lesson

For each group, gather the following materials:

- Dry-erase board, marker, and eraser (for you)
- Reading notebooks for student responses and new vocabulary (1 for each student. For information on how to create the notebooks, see the Teaching Tip! below.)
- Assessment kit, which includes leveled reading passages and comprehension questions
- Texts in a variety of genres
- Sticky notes (1-inch and 3-inch) and sticky flags
- Timer

Reproducibles on the CD/online:

- Assessment Summary Chart for Fluent Readers (several copies): A reproducible also appears on page 60.
- Fluent Guided Reading Lesson Plan (several copies): Reproducibles also appear on page 61–62.
- Character Trait Chart (1 for each student)
- Inference Cards (1 set for each student or a laminated teacher set on an O-ring)
- Scaffolds for Literal, Interpretive, and Evaluative Comprehension Strategies
- Rubric for Fluent Guided Reading Lesson (Levels Q and Above)

READING NOTEBOOKS I recommend reading notebooks where students can record their notes and responses during all components of the reading workshop. As a management tool, you can color-code each section as follows: white for recording responses from independent reading, yellow for whole-group lessons, pink for guided reading, and blue for new vocabulary.

SOME COMMONLY ASKED QUESTIONS

Should students write during the first reading of a text or after they read it?
Students should always write during the first reading of a text because it will improve their comprehension and help you evaluate their understanding. Furthermore, it lets you know how much scaffolding to give each student. Having students write after they read an entire selection can also be beneficial as long as you have a purpose for the assignment. Add guided writing after students read the text to provide writing support and extend comprehension.

Can students write on a whiteboard instead of in their reading notebooks? I have students write in their notebooks because their writing becomes an artifact you can use for evaluation. If students write on a whiteboard, you have no record of what they did.

Why should I teach students how to write in bullets? As I demonstrated in the model lesson on "Landslide Disaster!" writing in bullets helps students identify the most important information in a text. This process also prevents them from copying the text word for word.

What should I do while students are reading silently? You should have mini-conferences with each student. Look at their notes, ask if there was something that confused them, ask them a question about what they read, ask them to tell you what they are going to write next, help them write bullets, help them use vocabulary strategies, and so on.

What should I do if students cannot stay focused on their independent reading while I am teaching a guided reading group? If students do not enjoy independent reading, they either have not found a book they like, or the book they have chosen is too difficult. Have a class meeting and explain why students need to read for 20–40 minutes each day. Ask students to help you organize your classroom library so they can easily find books they might like. Do book talks and book teasers. Ask your librarian to pick out some really good books and put them in a box so students can access those texts. Once books are available and students realize that reading independently is the only thing they will be able to do during reading workshop, the vast majority will become eager readers. If this approach doesn't work, have students do three literacy activities during reading workshop, one of which is independent reading.

Model Lesson in Action:
Fluent Reader Level S—Fiction

Video Running Time: 23:40 | *scholastic.com/NSGRAction3UP*

In this video, I show what Day 1 of a fluent guided reading lesson at around Level S looks and sounds like. This group is composed of five students whose reading levels range from R to T. Some are English Language Learners (ELLs). They have a good grasp of the literal and interpretive levels of thinking but haven't yet mastered evaluative thinking. They've practiced analyzing character traits and are familiar with fables and fairy tales, so I chose the fable "The Lobster and the Crab" from Arnold Lobel's collection, *Fables*. The story's two well-defined characters will help students master the character analysis focus strategy.

Take a moment to look at the completed lesson plan below and then view Day 1 of the lesson in the video. I suggest you print the corresponding completed Fluent Guided Reading Lesson Plan available online and refer to it as you watch the lesson.

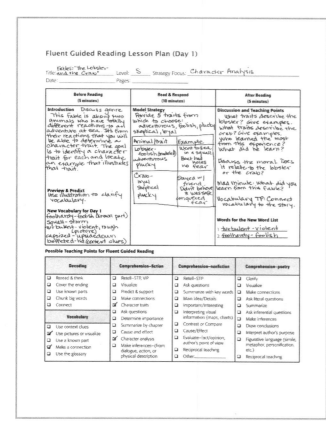

Day 1

BEFORE READING

To prepare for the lesson, I drew a two-column chart on the chalkboard with the following headers: *Character Trait* and *Example*. I also wrote the new vocabulary words from the fable on a whiteboard. As a scaffold, I wrote on a second whiteboard the five character traits I wanted students to use to describe the lobster and the crab.

INTRODUCTION

Gist Statement/Preview and Predict: Because I wanted to include genre discussion with my introduction, I began by discussing what students knew about fables. I introduced the text by asking them to identify the genre and then share some characteristics of a fable. As I revealed a little bit about the fable, I asked the students to identify each character in the illustrations in the text.

State the Focus Strategy: I explained the purpose of the lesson and showed students the Character Trait/Example chart that they would complete to link certain traits to each character.

New Vocabulary: Using a whiteboard, I displayed the new vocabulary words and used the four steps to introduce each one: say the word, give a simple definition, ask students to turn and talk to relate the word to their own experiences, and relate it to the text.

READ & RESPOND

Before having students read the fable, I restated the focus strategy so they would know what to do as they read, and I discussed the five traits they were to look for. Then students read silently. During my individual conferences, I asked students to read aloud so I could evaluate their decoding skills.

MODEL THE FOCUS STRATEGY After I worked individually with each student, I asked everyone to stop reading so I could model a response on the Character Trait/Example chart. As students worked on their charts, I jotted down my observations about their decoding skills and their ability to use the focus strategy.

AFTER READING

DISCUSSION AND TEACHING POINTS In our discussion of the fable, I asked students to match each trait to one of the characters and support their thinking with examples from the text. Then, to guide students to think more deeply (on the evaluative level), I asked, "Who do you think learned the most from this experience?" Because the students were thinking in only literal terms, I turned their attention to the moral of the fable. To expand on the moral, I assigned a Mad Minute and had students write for one minute about what they had learned from the fable. To close the lesson, I incorporated my vocabulary teaching point—make a connection—to two of the new vocabulary words.

Suggestions for supporting students at all three levels of comprehension appear on the Scaffolds for Literal, Interpretive, and Evaluative Comprehension Strategies form on the CD/website.

WORDS FOR THE NEW WORD LIST I had students add the words *turbulent* and *foolhardy* to their New Word List, explaining that they could use the content of "The Lobster and the Crab" to help them remember what these words mean.

DIFFERENTIATING INSTRUCTION Working with individual students allows me to differentiate my instruction. In this lesson, I taught the following strategies and skills: *reread to support comprehension, match character traits with actions, summarize, use text evidence for support, and ask an evaluative question to raise comprehension.* More information on some of these strategies appears on page 53.

NEXT STEPS

Because almost everyone handled the focus strategy well, I decided to change my original plan for Day 2. Instead of using another fable, "The Ducks and Fox," for more practice with character analysis, I created a new lesson plan for another genre and a new focus strategy: a nonfiction magazine article on landslides that would help students work on cause and effect. This new model lesson begins on the next page.

One student did need more scaffolding, so I scheduled an individual conference with her to work on character analysis. I used "The Ducks and the Fox" with this student. You can view this conference in the "Individual Conference: Struggling Reader" video. Details about it appear on pages 54–55.

My observations on Day 1 of the lesson are on the next page.

MY NOTES

Discussion and Teaching Points
Students demonstrated a literal understanding of the fable, referring explicitly to the text to support their answers. They had difficulty applying the moral of the story to situations outside the fable. More work is needed on interpretive comprehension.

Anecdotal Notes
I noted that most of the students understood character traits but needed support to elaborate on the connection between the character's action and the trait. I will weave this reading standard into whole-group instruction and future guided reading lessons. I also wrote a note about working on character traits with Cristal in an individual conference.

Mad Minute
These students responded to the lesson at a literal level. Most wrote about the dangers of going out to sea in a storm. Even though we discussed the moral prior to the Mad Minute, most of the students didn't grasp the concept. We should readdress the concept of central message, lesson, or moral during whole-group instruction and guided reading lessons.

Fluent Guided Reading Lesson Plan (Day 1)

Title: Fables: "The Lobster and the Crab"   Level: S   Strategy Focus: Character Analysis
Date: _____   Pages: _____

Before Reading (5 minutes)	Read & Respond (10 minutes)	After Reading (5 minutes)
Introduction Discuss genre This fable is about two animals who have totally different reactions to an adventure at sea. It's from their reactions that you will be able to determine a character trait. The goal is to identify a character trait for each and locate an example that illustrates that trait.	**Model Strategy** Provide 5 traits from which to choose: adventurous, foolish, plucky, skeptical, loyal	**Discussion and Teaching Points** What traits describe the lobster? Give examples. What traits describe the crab? Give examples. Who learned the most from this experience? What did he learn?

Animal/trait	Example
Lobster- foolish (model) adventurous plucky	Went to sea in a squall. Boat had holes. no fear
Crab- loyal skeptical plucky	Stayed w/ friend. Didn't believe it was safe. conquered fear

Preview & Predict
Use illustration to clarify vocabulary.

New Vocabulary for Day 1
foolhardy- foolish (known part)
squall- storm
turbulent- violent, rough (picture)
capsized - upsidedown
buffeted- hit (context clues)

Discuss the moral. Does it relate to the lobster or the crab?

Mad minute: What did you learn from this fable?

Vocabulary TP: Connect vocabulary to the story.

Words for the New Word List
1. turbulent - violent
2. foolhardy - foolish

Possible Teaching Points for Fluent Guided Reading

Decoding	Comprehension–fiction	Comprehension–nonfiction	Comprehension–poetry
☐ Reread & think	☐ Retell–STP, VIP	☐ Retell–STP	☐ Clarify
☐ Cover the ending	☐ Visualize	☐ Ask questions	☐ Visualize
☐ Use known parts	☐ Predict & support	☐ Summarize with key words	☐ Make connections
☐ Chunk big words	☐ Make connections	☐ Main Idea/Details	☐ Ask literal questions
☐ Connect	☑ Character traits	☐ Important/Interesting	☐ Summarize
	☐ Ask questions	☐ Interpreting visual information (maps, charts)	☐ Ask inferential questions
Vocabulary	☐ Determine importance	☐ Contrast or Compare	☐ Make inferences
☐ Use context clues	☐ Summarize by chapter	☐ Cause/Effect	☐ Draw conclusions
☑ Use pictures or visualize	☐ Cause and effect	☐ Evaluate–fact/opinion, author's point of view	☐ Interpret author's purpose
☐ Use a known part	☑ Character analysis	☐ Reciprocal teaching	☐ Figurative language (simile, metaphor, personification, etc.)
☑ Make a connection	☐ Make inferences–(from dialogue, action, or physical description)	☐ Other:_____	☐ Reciprocal teaching
☐ Use the glossary			

Model Lesson in Action: Fluent Reader Level S—Nonfiction

Video Running Time: 25:00 | scholastic.com/NSGRAction3UP

In this video, I show what a fluent guided reading lesson at around Level S looks and sounds like. This is the same small group I worked with in the previous model lesson for "The Lobster and the Crab." Since they finished reading that fable and demonstrated a good understanding of character analysis, I wanted this group to work with a different genre and another focus strategy. The text I selected was a magazine article called "Landslide Disaster!," by Bob Woods. It clearly states the reasons landslides occur, so it is ideal for teaching causes and effects.

Take a moment to look at the completed lesson plan below and then view Day 1 of the lesson in the video. I suggest you print the corresponding completed Fluent Guided Reading Lesson Plan from the website and refer to it as you watch the lesson.

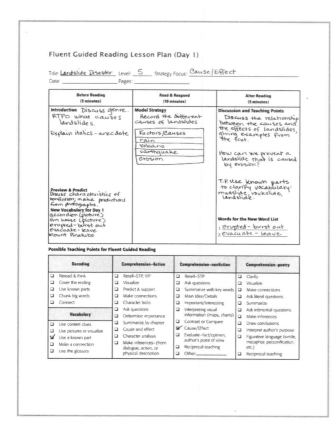

Day 1

BEFORE READING

To prepare for the lesson, I wrote the following question on the chalkboard: What <u>causes</u> landslides? Note that I underlined the word *causes* to scaffold students. I also wrote the new vocabulary words from the article on a whiteboard: *accordion, fun house, erupted,* and *evacuate.* To offer support for two of the new vocabulary words, I presented illustrations of an accordion and a fun house. In addition, I folded a piece of paper to create an accordion effect.

INTRODUCTION

I briefly reviewed the genre and focus strategy from the group's last lesson and then distributed the article "Landslide Disaster!" Students were able to identify the genre as nonfiction and point to characteristics of the text to support their responses.

Preview and Predict: The photograph of a landslide in the article offered a great opportunity to have students turn and talk to predict its cause.

State the Focus Strategy: I explained the purpose of the lesson, telling students that they would be reading the article to find out what causes landslides. I demonstrated how to use a bullet to record each cause.

New Vocabulary: On a whiteboard, I displayed the new vocabulary words and then used the four steps to introduce them: say each word, give a simple definition, ask students to turn and talk to relate the word to their own experiences, and relate it to the text. This is where I pulled out my props to help illustrate the meanings of *fun house* and *accordion*.

READ & RESPOND

Before having students read the article, I pointed out the italicized text in the beginning and explained that this was a way to highlight someone's true story. I also talked about some locations students might not have known. Then the students read the article silently.

MODEL THE FOCUS STRATEGY Despite the fact that I had modeled the focus strategy and showed them how to use bullets for each cause, I realized as I worked with students that they didn't understand the task. I then emphasized where the causes would be found—on the first page and under each heading. I also told them to write down details about each cause.

AFTER READING

DISCUSSION AND TEACHING POINTS As students discussed the causes in the article, I wrote each one beside a bullet on the chalkboard. Then I asked them to give details from the text to expand on each cause. To deepen their understanding of the article, I asked the following "how" question: How can we prevent landslides that are caused by erosion? I also drew a picture of a hillside to support students.

WORDS FOR THE NEW WORD LIST Students added *erupt* and *evacuate* to their New Word List. The lesson ended with the group acting out these words.

DIFFERENTIATING INSTRUCTION Working with individual students allows me to differentiate my instruction. In this lesson, I used the following strategies and skills: *define vocabulary and build comprehension, use prediction to reinforce comprehension,* and *ask "how" questions to deepen understanding.* More information on some of these appears on page 53.

NEXT STEPS

On Day 2, we will continue with the same text and focus strategy. Although students were able to easily identify causes, they relied too much on the text and had difficulty using inferential thinking to explain how the causes led to landslides.

My observations on Day 1 of the lesson are on the next page.

Fluent Guided Reading Lesson Plan (Day 1)

Title: _Landslide Disaster_   Level: _S_   Strategy Focus: _Cause/Effect_
Date: _____   Pages: _____

Before Reading (5 minutes)	Read & Respond (10 minutes)	After Reading (5 minutes)
Introduction Discuss genre. RTFO what causes landslides. Explain italics – anecdote	**Model Strategy** Record the different causes of landslides Factors/Causes rain volcano earthquake erosion	**Discussion and Teaching Points** Discuss the relationship between the causes and the effects of landslides, giving examples from the text. How can we prevent a landslide that is caused by erosion? T.P. Use known parts to clarify vocabulary: mudslide, rockslide, landslide.
Preview & Predict Discuss characteristics of nonfiction; make predictions from photographs. **New Vocabulary for Day 1** accordion (picture) fun house (picture) erupted – burst out evacuate – leave Mount Pinatubo		**Words for the New Word List** 1. erupted – burst out 2. evacuate – leave

Possible Teaching Points for Fluent Guided Reading

Decoding	Comprehension–fiction	Comprehension–nonfiction	Comprehension–poetry
☐ Reread & think	☐ Retell–STP, VIP	☐ Retell–STP	☐ Clarify
☐ Cover the ending	☐ Visualize	☐ Ask questions	☐ Visualize
☐ Use known parts	☐ Predict & support	☐ Summarize with key words	☐ Make connections
☐ Chunk big words	☐ Make connections	☐ Main Idea/Details	☐ Ask literal questions
☐ Connect	☐ Character traits	☐ Important/Interesting	☐ Summarize
	☐ Ask questions	☐ Interpreting visual information (maps, charts)	☐ Ask inferential questions
Vocabulary	☐ Determine importance	☐ Contrast or Compare	☐ Make inferences
☐ Use context clues	☐ Summarize by chapter	☑ Cause/Effect	☐ Draw conclusions
☐ Use pictures or visualize	☐ Cause and effect	☐ Evaluate–fact/opinion, author's point of view	☐ Interpret author's purpose
☑ Use a known part	☐ Character analysis	☐ Reciprocal teaching	☐ Figurative language (simile, metaphor, personification, etc.)
☐ Make a connection	☐ Make inferences–(from dialogue, action, or physical description)	☐ Other:_____	☐ Reciprocal teaching
☐ Use the glossary			

Advanced Fluent Lesson Highlights: Level U/V

Video Running Time: 8:19 | *scholastic.com/NSGRAction3UP*

In this video, I show highlights from Day 1 of a fluent lesson for advanced students. This group is composed of fourth graders reading at Level U/V. The text I chose is the short story "Thank You, Ma'm" by Langston Hughes. It will give students plenty of opportunities to use the focus strategy—making inferences—and strengthen their comprehension.

VIEW ONLINE ▶ Take a moment to look at the completed lesson plan below and then view the video. I suggest you print the corresponding completed Fluent Guided Reading Lesson Plan from the website and refer to it as you watch the highlights of the lesson.

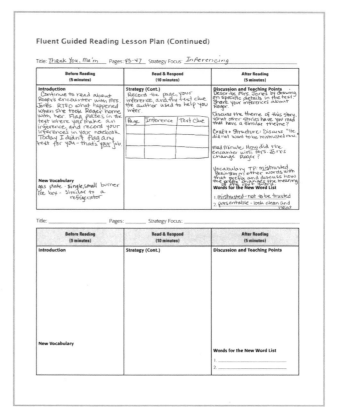

Before Reading

To prepare for the lesson, I placed flags in each student's copy of "Thank You, Ma'm" to mark places in the text where I wanted students to make an inference. To scaffold inferential thinking, I used a set of Inference Cards: Physical Traits, Dialogue, Action, and Inner Thoughts. I cut apart the sections on the Inference Cards reproducible, glued each one to an index card, laminated them, and organized them on an O-ring. I also wrote the new vocabulary words on a whiteboard. To model the strategy, I created the following chart:

Page	In the Book	In My Head

INTRODUCTION

Review: Even though these students were familiar with making inferences and using the Inference Cards, I still reviewed the process to refresh their memories.

Gist Statement: I gave a brief description of the story and the purpose for reading it.

Preview & Predict: I used an illustration in the story to preview the text and help students make predictions about it.

New Vocabulary: "Thank You, Ma'm" contains some time-period words that are seldom used today. I introduced them along with other words that did not have text support.

Read & Respond

MODEL THE FOCUS STRATEGY To model the focus strategy of inferencing, I read aloud the first paragraph of the story and thought aloud as I filled in the chart on the chalkboard. I recorded the page number, the portion of text that helped me make an inference, and the inference itself.

Page	In the Book	In My Head
40	walking alone	She's brave plucky (not afraid)

Students then read the text independently and silently, stopping to write an inference in their notebooks when they reached a flagged portion of text. I encouraged them to find other places in the text to make inferences. While the group read, I worked with individuals, differentiating my instruction based on the level of support each one needed.

AFTER READING

DISCUSSION AND TEACHING POINTS After students read for about 10–12 minutes, they shared the inferences they had made and told whether they used action, dialogue, physical traits, or inner thoughts to make the inference. Explaining the reason behind their thinking guides students to process at the evaluative level.

My teaching point—How do you think Mrs. Jones is going to change Roger?—guided students to make a prediction about what they might encounter in the text on Day 2.

WORDS FOR THE NEW WORD LIST I asked students to add the words *frail* and *barren* to their New Word List.

 CLOSING THE LESSON Always close a lesson by encouraging students to use the focus strategy when they are reading independently. Our goal is to have students employ strategies naturally as they read.

SUMMARY OF DAYS 2 AND 3

On Day 2, students continued to read "Thank You, Ma'm" and make inferences, but this time I didn't flag the text for them; I shifted the responsibility to the students. I introduced two time-period words: *gas plate* and *ice box*. As they read independently, I had individual conferences. In the discussion afterward, we talked about character description, inferences about a character, the story's theme, and craft and structure. I then assigned a Mad Minute activity. My teaching point on Day 2 focused on word analysis. After we discussed the affixes *mis-* and *-able*, students added two words from the story (*mistrusted* and *presentable*) to their New Word List.

My observations on Day 1 of the lesson are on the next page.

MY NOTES

New Vocabulary
It's easy to overlook words or concepts that are familiar to you but new to your students. Unless students are Elvis Presley or Carl Perkins enthusiasts, they've probably never heard of "blue suede shoes."

Fluent Guided Reading Lesson Plan (Day 1)

Title: Thank You Ma'm   Level: U/V   Strategy Focus: Inferencing

Date: _____   Pages: _____

Before Reading (5 minutes)	Read & Respond (10 minutes)	After Reading (5 minutes)
Introduction Review how to make an inference: dialogue, action, physical traits, inner thoughts. This story is about a young boy who tries to steal a woman's purse. RTFO how the woman influences the boy. **Preview & Predict** Discuss illustrations on p.41. **New Vocabulary for Day 1** blue suede shoes half-nelson — choke hold stoop — porch	**Model Strategy** w/ 1st paragraph As you read, notice where I placed a flag. Stop, think, and record your inferences. In at least one place, I want _you_ to flag the text where you made an inference. 	page	In the book	In my head
40	walking alone	brave, plucky		**Discussion and Teaching Points** Share inferences and discuss which text clue was used (action, dialogue, physical traits, inner thoughts). TP: How do you think Mrs. Jones might change Roger? Who is frail in the story? Why might the boy be frail? barren — context clues **Words for the New Word List** 1. frail - weak 2. barren - bare

Possible Teaching Points for Fluent Guided Reading

Decoding	Comprehension—fiction	Comprehension—nonfiction	Comprehension—poetry
☐ Reread & think	☐ Retell—STP, VIP	☐ Retell—STP	☐ Clarify
☐ Cover the ending	☐ Visualize	☐ Ask questions	☐ Visualize
☐ Use known parts	☐ Predict & support	☐ Summarize with key words	☐ Make connections
☐ Chunk big words	☐ Make connections	☐ Main Idea/Details	☐ Ask literal questions
☐ Connect	☐ Character traits	☐ Important/Interesting	☐ Summarize
Vocabulary	☐ Ask questions	☐ Interpreting visual information (maps, charts)	☐ Ask inferential questions
☑ Use context clues	☐ Determine importance	☐ Contrast or Compare	☐ Make inferences
☐ Use pictures or visualize	☐ Summarize by chapter	☐ Cause/Effect	☐ Draw conclusions
☑ Use a known part	☐ Cause and effect	☐ Evaluate—fact/opinion, author's point of view	☐ Interpret author's purpose
☐ Make a connection	☑ Character analysis	☐ Reciprocal teaching	☐ Figurative language (simile, metaphor, personification, etc.)
☐ Use the glossary	☑ Make inferences—(from dialogue, action, or physical description)	☐ Other:_____	☐ Reciprocal teaching

Discussion and Teaching Points
Students needed support to identify the text clue.

Anecdotal Notes
Only one student was successful in independently practicing the strategy. The others needed prompting to identify the text clue and/or elaborate on it.

Next Steps
Students demonstrated independence with the strategy during guided reading, so I will encourage them to practice the strategy during independent reading. Having them mark places in a text where they make inferences and writing about them in a weekly response letter to their teacher will be a good way to monitor and assess their understanding of the strategy.

Target Skills and Strategies

For more information on the following skills and strategies, see the "Teaching Points" video clips:

- **Monitor for Meaning and Cover the Ending to Decode a Word:** When they have difficulty decoding, remind students to ask themselves whether a word makes sense. In the video clip, covering the ending of *surprising* helped the student correct his miscue.

- **Define Vocabulary and Build Comprehension:** You can teach vocabulary and comprehension simultaneously; for example, ask students to compare and contrast terms as they summarize a passage.

- **Match Character Traits With Actions:** Throughout a text, a character commonly displays more than one trait. With prompting and practice, students become more adept at identifying which trait a character is revealing in a given situation.

- **Use Text Clues to Make Inferences:** Text-clue cards (Inference Cards) help students focus on a character's actions, dialogue, physical traits, or inner thoughts to make inferences.

- **Reread to Support Comprehension:** Asking students to reread to find examples in the text that support their response deepens comprehension.

- **Ask an Evaluative Question to Raise Comprehension:** You can carefully frame discussion questions that guide students to go beyond the text and think at the evaluative level.

REFLECTION

Take time to evaluate my model lesson plans. Based on what you saw, would you make changes in your lesson plan?

ACTION

▶ Complete the Rubric for Fluent Guided Reading Lesson to evaluate the components of each of my lesson plans.

▶ Review and refine your lesson plan.

▶ Teach your lesson. Remember to record your observations and notes to assess your students' performance and progress.

Individual Conference: Struggling Reader

Video Running Time: 6:34 | scholastic.com/NSGRAction3UP

During an individual conference, you can provide just the right amount of support, then gradually reduce that support until the student is independently applying the strategy.

 To see this process in action, watch the "Individual Conference" video. Cristal was in the small group that read the fable "The Lobster and the Crab" in the Level S Model Lesson in Action. After observing Cristal's difficulty with identifying character traits during the lesson, I decided to work one-on-one with her, using my plan for Day 2 of the group lesson. Working with "The Ducks and the Fox," another fable from the Arnold Lobel book, will give Cristal more practice with the character analysis strategy.

PREPARING FOR THE CONFERENCE Before meeting with Cristal, I narrowed down the character traits I wanted her to work with in this fable—*wise*, *foolish*, and *adventurous*—and wrote each word on a sticky note. I also created a T-chart on a whiteboard and labeled it with the characters "Duck #1" and "Duck #2" so Cristal could connect each trait with the correct character.

STATE THE STRATEGY FOCUS After explaining the purpose of the conference to Cristal, I retaught the strategy focus by having her think about each character's action to help her identify the trait the character is displaying.

DRAW ATTENTION TO AN ACTION My refrain for this conference was, "What did the character do?" Identifying the action would help Cristal identify the character trait.

OFFER LIMITED CHOICES TO HELP STUDENT FOCUS Since she correctly attached the word *adventurous* to Duck #1, I supported Cristal by offering only the two remaining choices to describe Duck #2: *wise* and *foolish*. Notice that when Cristal responded, I asked her to explain her thinking: "Why do you think it's foolish? Why would it be foolish to tell the fox they come along this road every day?"

READ AHEAD FOR EVIDENCE Making a prediction and reading ahead for evidence to confirm or revise helps the reader monitor for comprehension. In this conference, I asked Cristal to think about what might happen to the ducks if they went the same way they always did.

REVISIT AND REVISE PREDICTIONS (OR APPLY NEW INFORMATION TO AN EARLIER PREDICTION) After reading ahead, we stopped and I again asked Cristal whether the second duck was being wise or foolish. This time, she selected the correct character trait and was able to explain her thinking.

FOLLOW-UP

Cristal showed progress with my scaffolding, and I expect will show even more progress once she practices the strategy during independent reading. After an individual conference, continue to monitor the student's progress during subsequent guided reading group lessons.

The Fluent Guided Reading Lesson Framework: Addressing Standards

The chart below shows how each component of the Fluent Lesson Framework aligns with commonly held state and national standards.*

Fluent Lesson Component/ Objective	*Standards
Before Reading	
Introduction Preview & Predict New Vocabulary	**LITERATURE** **Integration of Knowledge and Ideas:** **4.7** Make connections between the text of a story and a visual presentation of the text, identifying where each version reflects specific descriptions and directions in the text. **5.7** Analyze how visual elements contribute to the meaning, tone, or beauty of a text. **INFORMATIONAL TEXT** **Integration of Knowledge and Ideas:** **4.7** Interpret information presented visually and explain how the information contributes to an understanding of the text in which it appears.
Read & Respond	
Model Strategy	**LITERATURE** **Key Ideas and Details:** **4.1** Refer to details in a text when explaining what the text says explicitly and when drawing inferences from the text. **4.2** Determine a theme of a story, drama, or poem from details in the text; summarize the text. **4.3** Describe in depth a character, setting, or event in a story, drawing on specific details in the text. **5.1** Quote accurately from the text when explaining what the text says explicitly and when drawing inferences from the text. **5.2** Determine a theme of a story, drama, or poem from details in the text, including how characters ina story or drama respond to challenges or how the speaker in a poem reflects upon a topic; summarize the text. **5.3** Compare and contrast two or more characters, settings, or events in a story, drawing on specific details in the text. **6.1** Cite textual evidence to support analysis of what the text says explicitly as well as inferences drawn from the text. **6.2** Determine a theme or central idea of a text and how it is conveyed through particular details; provide a summary of the text distinct from personal opinions or judgments. **6.3** Describe how a particular story's plot unfolds in a series of events as well as how the characters respond or change as the plot moves toward a resolution.

Craft and Structure:

4.4 Determine the meaning of words and phrases as they are used in a text, including those that allude to significant characters found in mythology.

4.6 Compare and contrast the point of view from which different stories are narrated, including the difference between first- and third-person narratives.

5.4 Determine the meaning of words and phrases as they are used in a text, including figurative language such as metaphors and similes.

5.6 Describe how the narrator's or speaker's point of view influences how events are described.

6.4 Determine the meaning of words and phrases as they are used in a text, including figurative and connotative meanings; analyze the impact of a specific word choice on meaning and tone.

6.5 Analyze how a particular sentence, chapter, scene, or stanza fits into the overall structure of a text and contributes to the development of the theme, setting, or plot.

6.6 Explain how an author develops the point of view of the narrator or speaker in a text.

Integration of Knowledge and Ideas:

4.7 Make connections between the text of a story and a visual or oral presentation of the text, identifying where each version reflects specific descriptions in the text.

5.7 Analyze how visual and multimedia elements contribute to the meaning, tone, or beauty of a text.

Range of Reading and Level of Text Complexity:

4.10 By the end of the year, read and comprehend literature, including stories, dramas, and poetry, in the grades 4–5 text complexity band proficiently, with scaffolding as needed at the high end of the range. **5.10** By the end of the year, read and comprehend literature, including stories, dramas, and poetry, at the high end of the grades 4–5 text complexity band independently and proficiently.

6.10 By the end of the year, read and comprehend literature, including stories, dramas, and poems, in the grades 6–8 text complexity band proficiently, with scaffolding as needed at the high end of the range.

INFORMATIONAL TEXT

Key Ideas and Details:

4.1 Refer to details and examples in a text when explaining what the text says explicitly and when drawing inferences from the text.

4.2 Determine the main idea of a text and explain how it is supported by key details; summarize the text. **5.1** Quote accurately from a text explaining what the text says explicitly and when drawing inferences from the text.

5.2 Determine two or more main ideas of a text and explain how they are supported by key details; summarize the text.

6.1 Cite textual evidence to support analysis of what the text says explicitly as well as inferences drawn from the text.

6.2 Determine the central idea of a text and how it is conveyed through particular details; provide a summary of the text distinct from personal opinions or judgments.

6.3 Analyze in detail how a key individual event or idea is introduced, illustrated, and elaborated in a text (e.g., through examples or anecdotes).

Craft and Structure:

4.4 Determine the meaning of general academic and domain-specific words and phrases in a text relevant to a grade 4 topic or subject area.

5.4 Determine the meaning of general academic and domain-specific words and phrases in a text relevant to a grade 5 topic or subject area.

6.4 Determine the meaning of words and phrases as they are used in a text, including figurative, connotative, and technical meanings.

6.5 Analyze how a particular sentence, paragraph, chapter, or section fits into the overall structure of a text and contributes to the development of the ideas.

6.6 Determine an author's point of view or purpose in a text and explain how it is conveyed in the text.**Integration of Knowledge and Ideas:**

4.7 Interpret information presented visually and explain how the information contributes to an understanding of the text in which it appears.

4.8 Explain how an author uses reasons and evidence to support particular points in a text.

5.8 Explain how an author uses reasons and evidence to support particular points in a text, identifying which reasons and evidence support which point(s).

6.8 Trace and evaluate the argument and specific claims in a text, distinguishing claims that are supported by reasons and evidence from claims that are not.

Range of Reading and Levels of Text Complexity:

4.10 By the end of the year, read and comprehend informational texts, including history/social studies, science, and technical texts, in the grades 4–5 text complexity band proficiently, with scaffolding as needed at the high end of the range.

5.10 By the end of the year, read and comprehend informational texts, including history/social studies, science, and technical texts, at the high end of the grades 4–5 text complexity band independently and proficiently.

6.10 By the end of the year, read and comprehend literary nonfiction in the grades 6–8 text complexity band proficiently, with scaffolding as needed at the high end of the range.

FOUNDATIONAL

Phonics and Word Recognition:

4.3, **5.3** Know and apply grade-level phonics and word analysis skills in decoding words.

Fluency:

4.4, **5.4** Read with sufficient accuracy and fluency to support comprehension.

After Reading

Discussion and Teaching Points • *Decoding* • *Vocabulary* • *Comprehension: fiction* • *Comprehension: nonfiction* • *Comprehension: poetry* Words for the New Word List	**LITERATURE** **Key Ideas and Details:** **4.1** Refer to details in a text when explaining what the text says explicitly and when drawing inferences from the text. **5.1** Quote accurately from the text when explaining what the text says explicitly and when drawing inferences from the text. **6.1** Cite textual evidence to support analysis of what the text says explicitly as well as inferences drawn from the text. **INFORMATIONAL TEXT** **Key Ideas and Details:** **4.1** Refer to details and examples in a text when explaining what the text says explicitly and when drawing inferences from the text. **5.1** Quote accurately from a text explaining what the text says explicitly and when drawing inferences from the text. **6.1** Cite textual evidence to support analysis of what the text says explicitly as well as inferences drawn from the text. **VOCABULARY ACQUISITION AND USE** **4.4** Determine or clarify the meaning of unknown and multiple-meaning words and phrases based on grade 4 reading and content, choosing flexibly from a range of strategies. **5.4** Determine or clarify the meaning of unknown and multiple-meaning words and phrases based on grade 5 reading and content, choosing flexibly from a range of strategies. **6.4** Determine or clarify the meaning of unknown and multiple-meaning words and phrases based on grade 6 reading and content, choosing flexibly from a range of strategies.
Guided Writing	**Range of Writing** **4.10, 5.10, 6.10** Write routinely over . . . short time frames (a single sitting or a day or two) for a range of discipline-specific tasks, purposes, and audiences.

*The Common Core State Standards are used here as a point of reference.

Assessment Summary Chart for Fluent Readers

Proficient (+) Partially Proficient (✓) Limited (-)

Name	Instr. Text Level	Self-Monitor and Decode	Vocabulary	Retell	Ask Questions	Main Idea/ Details	Evaluate	Summarize	Character Analysis	Infer	Other

Fluent Guided Reading Lesson Plan (Day 1)

Title: _____ Level: _____ Strategy Focus: _____

Date: _____ Pages: _____

Before Reading (5 minutes)	Read & Respond (10 minutes)	After Reading (5 minutes)
Introduction **Preview & Predict** **New Vocabulary for Day 1**	**Model Strategy**	**Discussion and Teaching Points** **Words for the New Word List** 1. _____ 2. _____

Possible Teaching Points for Fluent Guided Reading

Decoding	Comprehension–fiction	Comprehension–nonfiction	Comprehension–poetry
❑ Reread & think ❑ Cover the ending ❑ Use known parts ❑ Chunk big words ❑ Connect	❑ Retell—STP, VIP ❑ Visualize ❑ Predict & support ❑ Make connections ❑ Character traits ❑ Ask questions ❑ Determine importance ❑ Summarize by chapter ❑ Cause and effect ❑ Character analysis ❑ Make inferences (from dialogue, action, or physical description)	❑ Retell—STP ❑ Ask questions ❑ Summarize with key words ❑ Main Idea/Details ❑ Important/Interesting ❑ Interpreting visual information (maps, charts) ❑ Contrast or Compare ❑ Cause/Effect ❑ Evaluate—fact/opinion, author's point of view ❑ Reciprocal teaching ❑ Other:_____	❑ Clarify ❑ Visualize ❑ Make connections ❑ Ask literal questions ❑ Summarize ❑ Ask inferential questions ❑ Make inferences ❑ Draw conclusions ❑ Interpret author's purpose ❑ Figurative language (simile, metaphor, personification, etc.) ❑ Reciprocal teaching
Vocabulary ❑ Use context clues ❑ Use pictures or visualize ❑ Use a known part ❑ Make a connection ❑ Use the glossary			

Fluent Guided Reading Lesson Plan (Continued)

Title: _____ Pages: _____ Strategy Focus: _____

Before Reading (5 minutes)	Read & Respond (10 minutes)	After Reading (5 minutes)
Introduction **New Vocabulary**	**Strategy (Cont.)**	**Discussion and Teaching Points** **Words for the New Word List** 1. _____ 2. _____

Title: _____ Pages: _____ Strategy Focus: _____

Before Reading (5 minutes)	Read & Respond (10 minutes)	After Reading (5 minutes)
Introduction **New Vocabulary**	**Strategy (Cont.)**	**Discussion and Teaching Points** **Words for the New Word List** 1. _____ 2. _____

References

Berger, M. (1999). *Chomp! A book about sharks*. New York: Scholastic.

Hughes, L. "Thank You, Ma'm" in *Spotlight on . . . point of view* (Scholastic Inc., 2004).

Levine, E. (2007). *Henry's freedom box*. New York: Scholastic.

Lobel, A. (1980). *Fables*. New York: HarperCollins.

National Governors Association Center for Best Practices and Council of Chief State School Officers. (2010). Common Core State Standards for English Language Arts and Literacy in History/Social Studies, Science, and Technical Subjects. Washington D.C.: National Governors Association Center for Best Practices, Council of Chief State School Officers.

Richardson, J. (2009). *The next step in guided reading: Helping all students become better readers*. New York: Scholastic.

Richardson, J. (2016). *The next step forward in guided reading: An assess-decide-guide framework for supporting every reader*. New York: Scholastic.

Woods, B., "Landslide Disaster!" in *Nonfiction passages with graphic organizers for independent practice* (Scholastic Inc., 2004).

Notes